Food Floor: My Woodward's Days

FOOD FLOOR
My Woodward's Days

Margaret Cadwaladr

Madrona Books & Publishing

Published by Madrona Books & Publishing
Langley, BC

ISBN Book: 978-1-9995465-1-9
Hardcover book: 978-1-9995465-2-6
Electronic book: 978-1-9995465-3-3

Includes Index

Every reasonable effort has been made to trace copyright holders
and to obtain permission to reproduce the photographs or other images
used in this book. We apologize for any errors or omissions and
would be grateful to be notified at madronabooks@shaw.ca
of any corrections so future editions can be corrected.

Editor: Judith Brand
Book Design: John McKercher

Printed in Canada

Contents

Introduction

Images of the demolition and reconstruction of Woodward's store flicker by on a screen supported by a pedestal. It slows only to highlight the removal of the familiar red W that proudly stood on the roof, a symbol of the love many in Vancouver had for the department store.

I sit in the expansive atrium featuring the striking reverse image of the Gastown riot by artist Stan Douglas. A police horse charges the crowd, helmeted officers, batons in hand, push a long-haired man into the back of a paddy wagon. Two kids sit on the curb. Two cops drag another across the street while others hold the traffic. Red rafters and a glass roof echo the colours of the W sign that stands behind plexiglass on the outer courtyard to Simon Fraser University (SFU).

While Douglas's impressive art piece speaks to one event that happened near the site, it seems to me that the affection and nostalgia many in Vancouver had for the legendary department store is missing. These warm feelings exist not only for shoppers but also for its many employees. I felt a need to record my recollections of my times there.

I had known Woodward's all my life. I remember, as a child, taking the tram down Main Street with my grandfather. We would visit the hardware department then go down the wide steps to the grocery department and order cases of Carnation condensed milk, grapefruit juice and tins of food for Muggins the cat. The next day the blue Woodward's truck would deliver the order.

The atrium of the new Woodward's development. The project was completed in 2009.

My mother bought us running shoes and underwear at Woodward's $1.49 Day sales. Each Easter, I picked out a new party dress and hat there. At Christmas, we lined up with large groups of children to visit Santa Claus in Toyland. Our trip was proceeded by weeks of scanning the various Christmas catalogues that arrived at the door. We scrutinised Eaton's bigger and flashier catalogue but told Woodward's Santa our hopes and dreams for gifts under the tree. I have an image of a low white picket fence containing lines of restless kids waiting their turn to sit on Santa's knee. The Santa button and cardboard hat that ensued were prized possessions. Later, we took our own children to visit Santa at Woodward's.

As the writing progressed, there were several developments in the world around Woodward's. Ming Wo decided to close its doors on Pender Street after serving the community since 1917. Soon, the streets grew silent as COVID-19 forced the world to stay at home. One of the results was the closure of the Army and Navy Department Store, another iconic institution in the area. I hope my recollections and the accompanying images offer readers the pleasure of nostalgia as well as a record of the times portrayed in this book.

Woodward's revolving beacon, circa 1938.

A Brief History

In 1892, after Charles Woodward's first store in Ontario burned, he moved to Vancouver with his family and opened a store on Westminster Avenue, now Main Street. In 1903, he built a new, larger store at 101 West Hastings Street at the corner of Abbott and moved his business there. It was called Store #1, the name many former employees still use.

One of the signature features of the Woodward's building was its revolving red W that topped a scale model of the Eiffel Tower above the elevator shafts. It replaced the 48-inch-diameter revolving beacon whose light could be seen as far away as Abbotsford to the east and Vancouver Island to the west. In the early 1940s, the wartime government ordered it removed as a security risk. The revolving W was installed in 1955 and became the iconic symbol of the much-loved department store.

The original store was four storeys high but soon grew to six. With additional wings, it comprised 600,000 square feet. The chain, officially Woodward Stores Limited, was and is typically referred to as Woodward's. Eventually expanding to 26 stores, the largest chain of retail establishments in Western Canada, it built its reputation on a firm commitment to excellent customer service.

What is now called the Downtown Eastside was once an ancient cedar and Coastal Douglas-fir forest, for generations home

Woodward's was at the heart of the business and shopping district. The area began to decline after the streetcars stopped running in favour of sleek cream-coloured buses with rounded back windows and soft tires. The image above was the interurban tram that brought shoppers to the area. The image on the right was a Brill bus stopped in front of Woodward's on September 30, 1968.

In each photograph, an advertisement for Pierre Paris and Sons is visible. The store opened in 1907 and specialized in work boots for loggers, orthotics and other custom items. [Brill bus photo is by Steve Scalzo and used with permission of the Illinois Railway Museum Scalzo Photo Collection; Hastings Street 1931 CVA 99-2619.]

to the Musqueam, Squamish and Tsleil-Waututh Nations. Not long after colonization, the area around the store became known as Skid Row. Significant logging operations took place, and logs were transported on rough skid tracks along what is now Gore Street. As the city evolved, the area became the centre of the business and shopping district. The city hall was nearby and the first courthouse was at Victory Square.

The legendary Food Floor opened as a groceteria after the First World War. The concept was ground-breaking in that customers could wander up and down the aisles with carts and make their own selections. In earlier years, grocers at Woodward's and other stores were still behind a counter. By 1952, Woodward's Food Floor was known as the largest grocery store in the world.

This photograph was taken on May 6, 2020 during the COVID-19 pandemic. The normally busy street is quiet as businesses closed and the population was urged to stay at home.

In 1910, a single price sale—25¢ Day—was established. By the end of the Second World War, this had evolved into $1.49 Day. The famous and often copied sale sold everything from kids' running shoes to potting soil.

The writing below the Strathcona Hotel ad is still clearly visible.

The beloved Christmas displays, now on yearly exhibition at Canada Place, started in 1930 with mechanized teddy bears, dolls and elves. Toyland on the 6th floor was an annual destination for many Vancouver families.

The decline in the area began when the interurban tram line closed in the 1950s. The car was king, and suburban shopping malls sprang up. Many shoppers, however, continued to travel downtown to Woodward's, Fields and the Army and Navy, although the area had become somewhat rundown.

By the time I started working at Woodward's in 1967, the building was already about 65 years old, which was evident in its infrastructure. The floors on the Food Floor were uneven. A marble placed on the floor would surely have rolled to the corner. One cold winter, cashiers stood in doubled paper bags to keep their feet warm.

The single occupancy rooms in many nearby hotels had long been filled with low-income tenants, including loggers and

The Metropole Hotel at 310 Abbott Street was one of the many hotels in the area.

fishers from out-of-town camps. Each hotel had a large beer parlour, and alcohol and heroin were the drugs of choice. Things went downhill with the introduction of crack cocaine. At the time of writing, the situation had further evolved into a tragic public health emergency as drugs polluted with fentanyl entered the area already blighted with poverty and despair.

Woodward's operated from 1903 to 1993 at 101 West Hastings Streets. In 1989, the Food Floor was sold to Safeway and operated as IGA. When the chain went bankrupt in 1993, all the stores closed. Although many reopened as a Hudson's Bay or Zellers,

Store #1 remained empty and boarded up. At one-point, homeless squatters occupied the building, then a tent city grew under the awning of the once proud store.

After much debate, a new building complex with mixed housing, a campus of Simon Fraser University (SFU) and retail outlets was developed. In 2010, a new red W was installed on the project while the original rusts in the courtyard.

Woodward's Selected Chronology

1892 Charles Woodward established a department store at Main and Georgia Streets

1903 Store #1 at 101 West Hastings Street opened on November 4

1908 store expanded from 4 floors to 6

1910 peanut butter machine installed, first 25¢ Day

1919 self-serve Groceteria opened

1926 Edmonton store opened

1927 structure based on Eiffel Tower is built with revolving searchlight on top

1930/31 parking garage and underground pedestrian tunnel to Food Floor is built

1930 first Christmas display windows

1940 (circa) revolving beacon removed from tower

1948 Port Alberni store opens

1950 Park Royal store opens

1951 first $1.49 Day

1953 employee profit-sharing initiated

1955 on April 24, the last streetcar on Hastings Route was discontinued, and the area began to decline; New Westminster store opens at 612 6th Street; revolving W sign with 625 red light bulbs installed

1957 Charles "Chunky" Woodward becomes CEO; new parking garage and enclosed pedestrian bridge built

1959 Oakridge shopping mall opens

1967 a freeway system was proposed which would have resulted in the demolition of most of Chinatown and part of Gastown. The project was met with fierce opposition

1971 Gastown "smoke-in" and riot at Abbott and Cordova

1989 Food Floor sold to Safeway and operates as IGA

1990 Chunky Woodward dies

1992 100 years of operation is celebrated, Woodward's filed for bankruptcy

1993 Woodward's closed and its assets, including 26 stores, purchased by Hudson's Bay

2002 homeless people squat at the Woodward's site and tent city established

2006 all but heritage portion of store demolished

2009 occupancy permits granted on new mixed-use development

2010 W returns to skyline

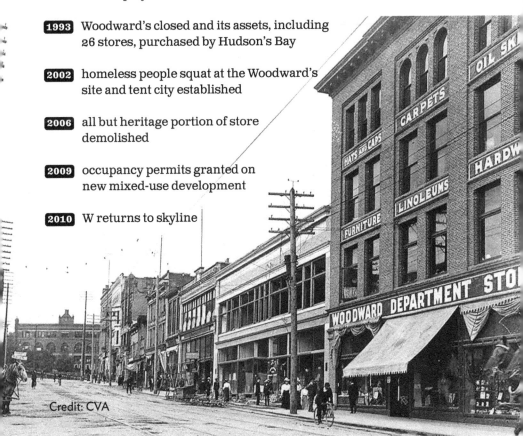

Credit: CVA

My Woodward's Days Begin

I started to work part-time at Woodward's in May 1967 while still going to school. Although the graduation ceremony took place that month, I had provincial exams to write. I didn't study as much as I should have, but low and behold, I won a scholarship to attend university. Although I did not have a specific career goal, I began my post secondary education with a full load of five courses, which I maintained until graduation in 1971, all the while working part-time at the store. My parents probably thought I would work for a few years, then marry and become a housewife. I picked out a full-length white lace grad gown with tiny green velvet ribbons down the back. When my mother saw my dress, she expressed surprise at my choice, but she reasoned it might serve as a wedding dress.

A wedding dress? I thought. I was only seventeen.

I cannot remember applying for the job or having an interview. I have a vague feeling that my mother might have seen an ad and suggested I apply. As I recall, the job offer came quickly. One day after school, I got a telephone message saying to be at the Food Floor later that week. I was joined by a tall blond girl, Leslie, who was also hired that day. We were introduced to Mr. Washburn, a shy mild-mannered man wearing a white jacket and a tie. He appeared to wear a toupee. He led us to an area

The courtyard of the new development showing the SFU campus.

out-of-bounds to the public behind swinging doors. Surrounded by skids of boxes and containers, he gave us a little pep talk and told us we were to start work on Friday evening.

But, I said, I am graduating from high school on Friday.

He paused and looked at me. Okay, you can start on Saturday, but don't let this happen all the time.

I rarely saw Mr. Washburn or Mr. Jewell, the other Food Floor manager. Faye Schuhart, Miss Schuhart to us, ruled the Food Floor from the Customer Service desk. She was a sturdy woman with back-combed hair in a French twist, her uniform strained across her chest. Woodward's prided itself on customer service and had high standards which were strictly enforced. Miss Schuhart was certainly as stern as any of the nuns I had encountered in school. I had the feeling, however, that she was fair, and in retrospect, she may also even have been quite shy.

Miss Schuhart stood on a raised podium, a clipboard and rotary telephone on the shelf behind her. As I stepped onto the Food Floor at the beginning of my shifts, she'd turn and silently look me up and down, presumably checking that my name tag was in place and my shoes polished, before giving me my assignment. Woodward's had a dress code. Chewing gum was forbidden, and an authorized name tag had to be worn. Miss Schuhart's job was to enforce the rules.

Woodward's

PRICES

On May 26, 1967, the day I started to work at Woodward's, evaporated milk sold at 6 cans for 95¢. "Mix or Match" canned cream corn, peas, green beans, mixed vegetables, Harvard beets or Boston baked beans sold for 6 for $1.00. Sixteen ounce loaves of Woodward's white or brown bread sold for 7 for $1.00. A 12 oz. basket of ripe strawberries was 25¢. An ad in the newspaper for Thanksgiving on October 2, 1968 listed:

Woodward's Supreme cranberry sauce 14 oz. tin 2 for 43¢

Woodward's Supreme Blend instant coffee 6 oz. jar 79¢

Woodward's Supreme pitted dates 15 oz. pkg. 2 for 45¢

Woodward's Supreme raisins 1 lb. cello 41¢

Woodward's Supreme Australian sultanas 4 lbs. 99¢

Woodward's Supreme apple juice 48 oz. tin 39¢

Frozen orange juice 4 for 79¢

Grade A fresh eggs 55¢ a dozen

Woodward's detergent 24 oz. 39¢

Grain-fed Alberta round roast 83¢ lb.

B.C. Grown Grade A turkey from 45¢ lb.

Grocery Wrapper

My first job was as a grocery wrapper. Today, this position is called grocery bagger, but in the earliest years of the store, groceries were wrapped in brown paper and tied with string. The name still stuck at Woodward's in the 1960s. All of the wrappers were young women working part-time; many were students.

The "boys" who worked on the Food Floor must have had a job title that was a mystery to me as they were always just referred to as "the boys." They moved carts, delivered change and ran multiple errands. They wore white aprons, ties and name tags, and like the grocery wrappers and some cashiers, many were students.

The job of a grocery wrapper was a more skilled task than one might imagine. Groceries going to the garage were packed in brown paper bags, then, two at a time, put into a foldable cardboard box and placed on a two-tiered metal cart. The groceries had to be very carefully packed, not only with the obvious considerations like cans on the bottom and eggs and tomatoes on top, but the whole thing had to be balanced in order to survive a journey to the parking garage on a conveyor belt that went under the street. Each bag had to be the same approximate weight and be light enough to handle. Watermelons and frozen turkeys needed special attention and sometimes were hand delivered to the garage. The large-scale use of plastic bags for groceries did not take place until late in the 1970s, but as I recall, paper bags

Credit: [CVA 779-E16.30]

Car park and walkway over Cordova Street circa 1981. The groceries travelled to the garage on a conveyor belt under the street.

still were preferred for shipping orders to the car park due to concerns about balanced loads.

Customers were given a small metal plate resembling a license plate. The matching one was clipped to the order with the customer's name written in thick black grease pencil, along with a notation of the order size, for example, 2 of 4. The totes were dispatched down an opening to the conveyor belt covered only by moveable flaps that would probably be prohibited as a safety hazard today.

If all these requirements were not met, the whole order could fall off the conveyor belt, causing the system to be shut down. Orders piled up in the store, and a traffic jam of waiting customers could develop in the garage. On more than one occasion, I was sent to a back room and down steep wooden steps to an area where cartons had fallen to form a muddle of smashed eggs, crushed tomatoes, pungent pickle juice and shattered glass jars. As I sorted and reassembled orders while cross-checking the

Credit: George Weinhaupf

Fishing boats in Coal Harbour circa 1969.

sales slips, the "boy" would have to run to the Food Floor getting replacement items.

Delivery orders were packed into fresh cardboard boxes assembled on the spot. The usual triplicate address label was attached by a clip. Perishables were given to the customer to take home. "Boys" would roll the carts away to a location I was not aware of.

A "special order" from a fishing boat was given priority treatment and a dedicated till. In the days before the glass towers of Coal Harbour, the fishing fleet tied up there. Fishermen came in to purchased extremely large orders that easily could comprise three or four shopping carts of goods: meats, dairy, canned goods, spices, condiments and all manner of items for an extended time at sea. Woodward's also sent mail orders up and down the coast and to remote communities, but these were not handled by the Food Floor grocery floor staff.

Butter Dreams

After a couple of months wrapping groceries, I was promoted to the position of cashier. Mr. Washburn took me aside and, in whispered tones, gave me a slip of paper indicating my promotion and raise in pay. I was trained with Violet Molnar, who stayed with the company for many years and became Miss Schuhart's associate.

Training consisted of seemingly endless mock transactions. There were no conveyor belts at the registers, instead they were what was called carousel-style. A load of groceries was placed on a shiny rotating metal tray, operated by pressing one's hip against a bar. Round it came: eggs, cans of peas and tubs of peanut butter. The tray was the only moving part of the check stand. These must have been remarkably well engineered and maintained as I don't recall them ever breaking down. We spent days ringing in sample orders and then pushing the groceries down a smooth metal path to the wrapping area. Ringing? As I write, I think this was probably a reference to the noise of the cash register without the constant beep of scanners.

We learned to handle different transactions: cash, cheque, credit, delivery and garage orders. Bills were always placed on the till shelf and change counted out loud and placed in the customer's hand before the transaction was complete and the customer moved on. The cash register did not calculate change; we made the calculation using brain power.

Our float consisting of $5, $2 and $1 bills as well as rolls of quarters, dimes, nickels, and pennies. There were no loonies and no toonies at that time. Fifty-cent pieces and silver dollars were not uncommon. Most people wrote cheques or used cash. Credit cards were still new. Credit cards courtesy of Barbara Mathias and Judith Brand.

There were no scanners. Cans were individually stamped with prices before they were put on the shelf. We had to memorize the price of many goods, especially those that could not be easily stamped. Butter, butter, butter. There were several types of butter: salted and unsalted, Woodward's brand, domestic and imported varieties. After practicing all day, I would go home tired and dream about pounds of butter and making change.

Cordova Street near the entrance to the parking garage between 1972–74.

Although, in many ways, the work of a cashier has not changed over the years, there have been many developments. Big-box stores like Walmart and Costco did not exist. There were no cell phones, barcodes, surveillance cameras, Facebook, Internet or self-checkouts. Tap technology was far in the distant unimagined future. A driver's license number was checked and recorded on the back of each cheque. The cashier placed charge cards in a long-handled contraption resembling an embossing seal and very carefully and precisely lined up the card then grasped the handle and firmly pressed down to make triplicate copies on thin sheets of paper with carbon.

Each of the large electric National Cash Registers (NCR) had two drawers, and you kept your tray with you all day, carrying it from register to register if you were doing relief. When the total button was pressed, the drawer opened with a surge of mechanical force that took awhile to get used to. We made all calculations including exchange rates for American tourists in our heads. Math was never my favorite subject, but I became a wiz at these.

Each register had two rolls of paper: one made a customer receipt, the other an internal record. Each new roll had to be carefully threaded through multiple rollers, and you hoped to have a patient customer standing next in your line. You knew the roll was coming to an end when you saw pink ink appear.

Another world existed behind swinging doors with windows to avoid collisions. Boxes were stacked high, and the smell of cardboard and produce permeated the air. Lettuce was trimmed with large knives, swish. The generators of large walk-in coolers hummed. There was a room with built-in stands where, after our shifts, we counted the money from our till and recorded totals in columns. If they were not busy near end of the day, most cashiers had already counted bills. The money was placed in heavy cloth bags and deposited with Dot, the woman in the glassed-in cash desk.

Shift begins

I would take the bus to work, pick up a freshly laundered and heavily starched uniform from the Food Floor, then move to the changeroom on the third floor and slap a coat of liquid polish on my white duty shoes. The polish was still drying as I ran to punch

This photograph was taken at the Park Royal Food Floor in 1950. Fashion had changed a great deal by the 1960s, but not at Woodward's, at least not on the downtown Food Floor. The only change to the uniform appears to be the addition of royal blue piping around the collar. My uniform was long enough to fall well below my knees.

While I attended UBC, I took the bus or walked across the old Cambie Street bridge. Sawmills were still active in the area and the air smelled of sawdust. Streetcar tracks were embedded in the roadway. There was no BC Place or Granville Island Market. The Woodward's W is visible near the Sun Tower at the corner of Pender and Beatty.

a cardboard timecard into a grey metallic mechanical time clock with a loud snap and hurry back down the escalator to the Food Floor. Then I would walk through the produce department with paper and pencil to write down specials for the week. Although a clerk weighed some items in the department, marking the price on the paper bag, we calculated the cost of many in our heads.

The Best of Everything

I came from a home where my mother cooked well-done roast beef and mashed potatoes for Sunday dinner, sometimes with Yorkshire pudding. My father's conservative tastes meant spaghetti and meatballs were the limit of ethnic cuisine. If pizza was popular, we didn't eat it.

We rarely went to restaurants aside from an occasional trip to the White Spot, but I think this was not unusual. Fast-food restaurants that are seemingly ubiquitous today did not exist. The first McDonald's restaurant opened in Canada on June 1, 1967, just as I started to work at Woodward's. At the time, processed foods were coming onto the market. I remember the amazement I felt when a friend's mother heated frozen TV diners for a family meal.

At the time, small corner stores still operated throughout the city. Supermarkets were common but much smaller than the Food Floor that had a cornucopia of ethic foods and gourmet items not available anywhere else. Woodward's was well-known and treasured for having a huge selection of foodstuff from all over the world. While many of these foods are now available in grocery stores, they were not at the time.

There were large round wheels of Scandinavian rye crackers, saffron and pistachios and matzo. Dolmas and olives were imported from Greece. Mona Brun, in *Cooking with Mona: The Original Woodward's Cookbook* (pages 16–17) added several exotic treats

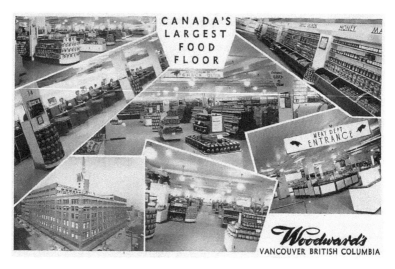

Canada's Largest Food Floor. Woodward's postcard circa 1953.

including "snails from France, rattlesnake meat from Florida and pappadams from India."

The store stocked 160 varieties of cheese from several countries: brie, camembert and Roquefort from France; Greek feta cheese, Danish Havarti and Tilsit, red wax-covered Gouda, Italian mozzarella and Swiss chesses. Each was cut by a clerk, weighed, wrapped in waxed brown paper and marked with the price.

I don't recall selling rattlesnake, but several meat cutters stood on sawdust floors behind long glass cases. Customers could order custom cuts of premium meats, poultry, foie gras, sausages and so on. Beef came from wholesalers as front and hind quarters. All cutting, trimming and grinding was done onsite. Meat cutters wearing white jackets and ties cut, weighed and wrapped selections at the counter.

When I was a child, we ate apples, oranges and bananas. Pineapple was usually in a can. Some foods that are common today like avocadoes and garlic cloves were unheard of or rare before waves of immigrants arrived from different parts of the world.

The popularity of Julia Child's cookbooks and television program helped to expand tastes in food.

The produce department was extensive and had foods that were exotic before the days of a globalized food supply: artichokes, papaya and passion fruit, pomegranate, mangos and star fruit. Some fruits and vegetables were placed in paper bags, and a clerk weighed and priced them in the produce department. If a customer failed to have their produce weighed, the item had to be sent back. The customer likely received subtle frowns by other customers in the line. We memorized the prices of others and calculated their cost in our heads.

At that time, Mandarin oranges, commonly referred to as Japanese oranges, were only available at Christmas. Their arrival at the port on ships from Japan was noted in the newspapers and heralded the beginning of the Christmas season. The fruit was wrapped in thin green paper in small wooden boxes. They were rare enough that Santa Claus would put one in our Christmas stocking.

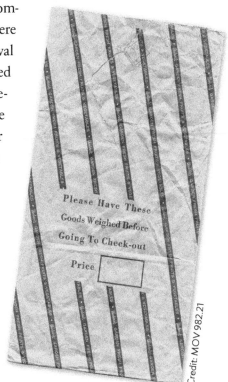

Credit: MOV 982.21

SIXTH FLOOR

Paint Centre • Wallpaper • Major Appliances • Toys • Music Centre •
TV Centre • Entertainment Accessories. In later years, a discount center

FIFTH FLOOR

Furniture • Floor Coverings

FOURTH FLOOR

Draperies • Staples • China • Glassware • Silverware • Giftware • Pictures
and Mirrors • Lamps • Hearing Aid Centre • Fabric Centre • Trim-a-Home

THIRD FLOOR

Woodward's Fashion Centres • Millinery • Ladies' Dresses •
Ladies' Sportswear • Ladies' Suits • Ladies' Coats • Ladies' Rainwear •
Custom Size Sportswear • Custom Size Dresses • Fur Salon •
Cosmopolitan Shop • Shop International • Chandelier Room
Young Vancouver Shops Junior Dresses • Junior Sportswear •
Junior Coats • Needlework • Portrait Studio • Gift Bazaar

SECOND FLOOR

Ladies' Shoes • Young Boutique Shoes • Lingerie • Foundations •
Children's Wear • Children's Shoes • Boys' Wear • Girls' Wear •
Teen 'n Twenty Shops Sporting Goods • Housewares • Kitchenware •
Appliance Accessories • Fireplace Accessories • Electricals • Luggage

MEZZANINE

Coffee Shop

MAIN FLOOR

Jewellery • Watches and Clocks • Handbags • Gloves • Cosmetics •
Women's Accessories • Neckwear • Blouses • Sweaters • Men's Wear •
Men's Clothing • Young Men's Shop • Men's and Boy's Shoes • Notions •
Stationery • Books • Candy • Drugs • Cameras • Hardware •
Auto Accessories

LOWER MAIN FLOOR

Woodward's Food Floor • Produce • Grocery • Candy • Bakery • Meat •
Flowers • Malt shop • Parcel Check • Restaurant • Tobacco Dept.

Woodward's Own Brands

Woodward's had a large selection of goods bearing its own brand, some from local suppliers with the Woodward's label added. They were known as high-quality items sold at a fair price. There was a long list of items: spices, jams, canned fruits and vegetables, cleaning products, frozen fish and meats, fruit juices, bakery products baked onsite, milk, eggs and butter, candies and chocolates.

FANCY GRADE

Woodward's SUPREME BRAND
TOMATO JUICE

5.5 fl oz
156 ml

Woodward's had a huge selection of their own brands.

12 FLUID OZS.

PACKED FOR
Woodward's
HEAD OFFICE
VANCOUVER, CANADA

Woodward's SUPREME BRAND
PURE GREENGAGE JAM

One of the favorites was Woodward's peanut butter that was roasted and ground onsite and packed into both jars and cans. It was smooth or crunchy, salted or unsalted and was a staple with many families. As a nod to its popularity, the new Nester's Market at the current Woodward's site continues to produce and sell a variety of Woodward's peanut butter.

Photo of spice jars: Lynda Welch

Woodward's

MAKING PEANUT BUTTER
by Robert McLachlan

I worked at Woodward's until the 100-year-old machine that made their peanut butter was retired, along with Clyde Turner who operated it. I made the peanut butter too. The recipe was simple. Chinese, not Texan, peanuts were used (for price and quality—we are talking 1977 here). They were roasted in a coffee roaster. Clyde roasted them darker to get more flavour than the other "natural" competitor, Sunny Jim. They were cooled by fan and then blanched—from there straight to a grinder where a primitive sifter shook salt into the hopper. The peanut butter came out a big spout and was bottled or canned by hand. That was the recipe: peanuts, salt.

Unless it was unsalted. Which no one bought, but we made anyway.

I made a short film about it that launched my film career. It was financed by my grocery stocking and peanut butter making career. The end.

Payday

Wages were good. Several of the older cashiers were shareholders in the company and explained that wages were good to keep unions out. Loyalty to the store was strongly encouraged. The company promoted a "family feeling," and there were several social events outside the workplace, including picnics at Bowen Island. I suspect they were probably more available to full-time staff than part-timers. I went roller-skating with a group from the Food Floor, attended weddings and made friends. I even shared an apartment with one of the wrappers and carpooled to university with another cashier.

I generally worked Friday evenings and Saturdays. Before the Lords Day Act was struck down by the courts in the 1980s, it was illegal to conduct retail business on Sundays. So, Woodward's, like other retail outlets in Canada, was closed on Sunday. We did summer vacation relief as well. I made enough money to pay my own way through university with occasional bursaries and a small student loan.

Staff at Woodward's were paid in cash in small brown envelopes. Wages were relatively good in efforts to keep unions out. Pay stub from 1968 courtesy of Lynda Welch (Walton).

30

Vancouver Sun classified ads for 1967 listed jobs for a hospital orderly position at $371 per month and $300 for an experienced secretary. An "attractive senior receptionist" could land a job for $325. Based on a 40-hour workweek, these folks were averaging $2.07 per hour. I remember making $3 per hour as a cashier, and a pay stub from Lynda Welch confirms wrappers started at $2.

Our earnings were paid in cash in small brown envelopes passed out from the glass cash window on the Food Floor. If money or other items were found and turned in to Lost and Found, they were given to the employee after a period, perhaps 90 days. On more than one occasion, I got another surprise brown envelope with the money I had turned in.

The Beacon

The Beacon, the in-house newsletter, was full of stories of promotions, engagements, picnics, marriages, births, retirements and deaths. It gave advice and even directives on proper grooming and the importance of good penmanship. They were readily available in the staff cafeteria and lounge but held little appeal to me as a part-time weekend teenage worker, but in retrospect they chronicled the store and the people who worked there.

Woodward's stores were loved by most employees. Regular ones were eligible for medical benefits, holidays, a pension and a profit-sharing plan. For the most part, there was a great deal of loyalty to, and affection for, the store.

All employees, including us part-timers, received a 15% discount. Parcels staff purchased were stamped with the receipt, stapled shut and retrieved at the end of the day. Receipts were then gathered and turned in to a cash desk. Shortly the discount, in cash, was returned in a small brown envelope. At my first Christmas, I bought my parents a large painting that stayed on their dining room wall for over forty years.

Shoppers

Shoppers from all parts of the city were loyal regulars. I came to recognize some of the names of Friday night customers. Others only came to the store at Christmas or as a destination for $1.49 Day. Hastings Street was also a prime street for various parades. The PNE parade was a huge annual event that drew many to the downtown core. Floats, bands, clowns, soldiers, sailors and marching bands filed past streets filled with enthusiastic crowds. I can vividly recall standing at the back of the throng on my lunch break. After the parade, many flooded into the store to do their shopping.

While large family orders were sent to the six-storey car park across Cordova Street, elderly shoppers tended to buy delivery orders loaded into foldable cardboard boxes. Their perishable items were packed in bags for them to take home.

Those living in cheap hotels and rooming houses SROs were mainly male seasonal loggers and fishers and Second World War vets. Most of these locals used the express checkouts as they bought few items at a time. They lived without proper refrigeration in their small spaces.

Customers were usually polite and patient. One day, however, there was a long line at my till. I sensed some impatience. A fellow came along in a crumpled suit, his fedora low on his face. He pushed his items ahead of him. In my usual practice, I placed the bill on the shelf of my tray and made his change. Once I put

Credit: CVA 180-1935

Other busy days were when the PNE parade went by on a Saturday at the beginning of August. Hastings Street was full of crowds. I remember going out onto the street and watching the parade on my lunch break, standing at the back of the crowd. Customers spilled into the store after the parade passed. In this image, Woodward's and other stores in the area are clearly visible. The tram tracks in the pavement are also visible in this 1953 photo.

the bill away and closed the drawer, he started to yell, saying he had given me a $20 bill and I had given him change for a ten. I stepped back and barely missed his fist as he swung at me. He must have already been under surveillance because he was swiftly and discreetly escorted away, presumably by the plainclothes loss prevention officers who were a constant presence. I was still shaking when I had my break.

Bea Wright's Kitchen

On occasion, I was asked to cover coffee breaks in Bea Wright's Kitchen. It was terrifying. The test kitchen and information booth were in a small office with a window at the back of the Food Floor. I dreaded hearing the phone ring, fearing someone would ask a question that I could not answer. I gained confidence when someone asked a question that I could answer from years of helping my mother in the kitchen. My main function was, however, to take telephone messages, presumably for Mona Brun, the Food Floor's well-known food consultant. There were no message machines, just little pink pads of paper to record the time and date of a call, a message and a telephone number.

Sometimes a customer would come to the kitchen. Thankfully, there were stacks of three-hole punched information and recipe sheets in slots against the wall, and often I could quickly find the recipe sheet.

Woodward's Recipes
From Bea Wright's Kitchen

32 W   FRUIT GALORE

CANNING PEACHES

Fully ripened peaches have the best flavor, and are the easiest to handle. Wash and peel. For fast action, add ½ c. Calgon per gallon of boiling water, and blanch peaches for approximately 2 – 3 minutes. Remove and immerse for 5 minutes in cold water, containing 2 tsp. Calgon per gallon – remove skins by hand; there should be no tearing of the fruit flesh. After peeling, halve the peaches and remove stones. To prevent browning, drop into weak salt water – 1½ tsp. salt to 1 qt. water. Prepare just enough for 3 qts. at a time, then pack before you peel more. Or, to prevent browning, for each quart of fruit, dissolve 1 tsp. ascorbic acid (or fruit saver), in ¼ c. cold water and sprinkle over prepared fruit.

HOT PACK – Use standard canning equipment and follow directions *closely and accurately.*

A medium syrup is satisfactory – 3 c. sugar to 6 c. water. For the first quart, place about 2 c. of hot canning syrup to a kettle. Rinse and drain 16 – 18 halves; put into hot syrup and boil 3 – 5 minutes. Pack hot in clean sterilized jars; fill with syrup ½'' from top. Wipe rim with a clean, damp cloth; put lid on as directed by manufacturer and set in warm place. For each additional jar add ¾ c. canning syrup and 16 – 18 halves to peach syrup remaining in kettle. Continue until as many jars are packed as water bath kettle will hold.

While packing jars, heat water in water bath kettle (canner). Place jars in boiling water or a rack which keeps them about ½'' from bottom. Add boiling water to bring level 1'' over jar tops. Process (heat) 20 minutes counting time from minute water boils. Remove jars at once; cool on rack away from drafts; complete seal if lids require it.

COLD PACK – Prepare fruit similar to Hot Pack directions. Pack into hot clean sealers in overlapping layers. If using halves, pack rounded side up, leaving ½'' headspace. Cover to within 1½'' of top of jar with boiling syrup. Seal jars and process in hot water bath, allowing 20 minutes for pints, 25 minutes for quarts.

WATER PACK – For water pack, pre-cook for the same length of time in plain water and fill packed jars with this hot water. Process as above.

PEACH JAM

Peel and cut well ripened peaches into small pieces. Put into large kettle without the addition of water. Cook slowly about 20 minutes or until peaches are soft enough to mash. Measure peach pulp and for each cup add 1 cup sugar. Return to heat and cook until desired consistency (about 20 minutes). Pour into hot sterilized jars and seal while hot.

FREEZING PEACHES

(Hale, Vedette, Veteran, Valiant, Rochester, Elberta) Ascorbic acid (Vit. C, and also known as fruit saver) is added to sugar syrups or cold water to preserve fresh color and flavor in fruits.

Syrup Pack -- add ½ tsp. ascorbic acid to each qt. of syrup – 3 c. sugar to 4 c. water; the syrup must be cold and the ascorbic acid added just before pouring over fruit. 1 qt. syrup will cover about 8 pint cartons.

With No Sugar – (For special dishes) – fruit packed in cold water, using 1 tspl ascorbic acid to each qt. of cold water.

Freeze soft, ripe fruit with a firm, fine-grained flesh; sort, wash, pit and peel (see above).

Use a syrup pack – start with ½ c. syrup in pint container, put peaches directly into syrup, slices, halves or quarters; add syrup to cover. Crumpled paper such as saran under the lid will keep fruit submerged. Leave ½'' headspace and freeze immediately.

FREEZER PEACH OR APRICOT JAM

3 c. prepared peaches, 5 c. sugar, 1 tbsp. ascorbic acid, 1 tsp. lemon juice, 1 pkg. Certo fruit pectin crystals, ¾ c. water.

PEEL and pit the peaches; mash and measure out 3 cups. Combine sugar and ascorbic acid, add to peaches with lemon juice and let this mixture stand 20 min. Cook pectin and water together to the boiling point; boil hard 1 min.; add to peach mixture and stir 2 min. (correct timing is important) . Ladle jam into sterilized jars; cover and let stand at room temperature. 24 hours. If using liquid pectin, stir in 1 bottle after mixture has been standing 20 min. Stir for 3 min., then pour into sterilized jars; let stand 1 or 2 days, until firm. Put on lids or tie on aluminum foil covers – paraffin will shrink during freezing, leaving the jam unprotected.   9 6-oz. glasses.

Bea Wright's Kitchen provided advice on cooking. There was a huge seasonal selection of recipes and advice.

Woodward's

Recipes

From Bea Wright's Kitchen

3W SALAD TIME

CAESAR SALAD 4 to 6 Servings
1 clove garlic, 1/2 cup olive oil, 1 cup 1/2 inch French bread, cubed, 3/4 tsp. salt, 1/4 tsp. dry mustard, 1/4 tsp. freshly ground pepper, 1 1/2 tsp. Worcestershire sauce, 6 anchovy fillets, drained and chopped, 2 tbsp. lemon juice, 1 egg, 1 large head romaine lettuce, washed, dried.
Crush 1/2 clove garlic and combine with oil in a covered jar. Let stand 1/2 hour. Heat 2 tbsp. of the oil-garlic mixture in a skillet. Saute crustless bread cubes until brown. Set aside. To remaining oil-garlic mixture, add salt, mustard, pepper, Worcestershire sauce, anchovies and lemon juice. Shake well. Just before serving, rub the inside of salad bowl with remaining 1/2 clove of garlic; discard. Cut coarse ribs from romaine lettuce and tear into bite-sized pieces in salad bowl. Shake dressing and pour over, then break the egg on top, toss well. Sprinkle with cheese, toss again. Sprinkle bread cubes over top of all and toss again.

SHRIMP SALAD 6 Servings
2 cups cooked shrimp, (2 - 5 oz. cans), 1/2 c. diced red-skinned apple, 1/2 c. celery leaves, 1/4 c. diced green pepper, 1/2 tsp. salt, 1/2 tsp. curry powder, if desired, 1/4 c. mayonnaise or salad dressing, lettuce cups.
Combine shrimp with apple, celery leaves and green pepper; add salt and curry powder to salad dressing. Combine and toss lightly. Serve in chilled lettuce cups.

CRAB SALAD 4 - 6 Servings
6 1/2 oz. can crab meat or equivalent in fresh, 3 c. shredded lettuce or spinach, 1 c. chopped celery, 2 hard cooked eggs, chopped, 1/3 c. mayonnaise, 3 tbsp. chili sauce, salt and pepper.
Distribute crab meat over surface, after tossing remaining ingredients.

CRAB SALAD SUPREME 6 Servings
1 c. flaked crab meat, 1/2 tsp. salt, 2 c. cubed pineapple, 2 tbsp. lemon juice, 2 bananas, 1/2 c. diced celery, 1/4 c. salad dressing.

To crab meat, add salt and rest of ingredients except mayonnaise. Mix well, then fold in mayonnaise.

WALDORF SALAD 6 Servings
1 c. diced celery, 1 c. diced apple, 1 c. seedless grapes, 1 c. raisins, 1/2 c. chopped walnuts.
Combine all with 3/4 c. mayonnaise or salad dressing and serve on lettuce leaves.

MACARONI SALAD Serves 4
1 c. elbow macaroni or small shells, 1 c. bias-cut celery, 1/3 c. chopped green pepper, 2/3 c. cubed sharp cheddar cheese, 1/4 c. finely chopped green onions, 2 tbsp. chopped pimiento, 1/3 c. mayonnaise, 1 tbsp. vinegar, 1/2 tsp. prepared mustard, 1/3 c. milk, 1/2 tsp. salt, dash pepper, 1/2 c. chopped ripe olives.
Cook macaroni in boiling salted water according to package directions; drain; rinse very thoroughly with cold water. In a large bowl combine macaroni, celery, green pepper, cheese, green onions and pimiento. In a small bowl combine thoroughly mayonnaise, vinegar, mustard, milk, salt, pepper and olives. Toss dressing gently with macaroni mixture. Line bowl with lettuce leaves, arranging salad on top. Garnish with parsley and hard cooked egg slices or wedges.

GREEK FETA CHEESE SALAD
3 tomatoes, cut in wedges, 1 cucumber, sliced, 1 onion, sliced, 2 green peppers, cut in rings, 6 tbsp. olive oil, 2 tbsp. wine vinegar, salt and pepper, pinch of oregano, 1/3 lb. Feta Cheese, 2 doz. black olives, chopped parsley.
Place prepared vegetables in a large bowl. Shake the olive oil, vinegar, salt, pepper, oregano together. Pour over salad. Refrigerate for at least 1 hour. Toss again, top with Feta cheese, (cut in squares) and the olives. Sprinkle with parsley.

THE LONG LASTING CABBAGE SALAD
Shred whole head of cabbage (Or red and green, if you wish). Separate 2 large onions into rings. In a large glass bowl, put a layer of cabbage and a

Break Time

After standing in one place for hours, with the repeated movements of sliding groceries, packing bags, tending the till, making change and filling out forms it was a relief to collapse into a chair and relax on our break. In retrospect, it must have been a difficult job for the many older women who worked on the Food Floor. I remember one telling me she had been at the store since the 1920s.

Operator-controlled elevators with glass doors and metal gates were still in use. The attendant announced the floors, pulled the brass handles to open the grate, then carefully adjusted the elevator level to prevent tripping. I rarely used these, preferring to ride the escalators, bounding two steps at a time, all the way to the top floor and back.

Rather than going to the staff cafeteria, I had lunch with one of the other cashiers in the restaurant. If I wanted a quiet place of refuge, I would go by myself to the small café on the mezzanine above the Book Shop. The eatery featured shrimp sandwiches on toasted cheese bread that had a pinch of paprika and featured tangy seafood sauce with a generous hint of horseradish.

Up on the roof was another refuge, an employee rest area. It was possible to sneak up and find myself alone. In summer, I would sometimes get something from the snack bar and head up there. The patio had views of the North Shore mountains and

Credit: VPL 26713

Escalators in the store circa 1945.

harbour. The sound of "O Canada" from giant horns on top of the BC Hydro building could be heard at noon.

Coffee breaks on busy Friday nights came late. Miss Schuhart would arrange the schedule so that all the young people could socialize in the lower restaurant area. The hostess, knowing we were on our short break, would quickly usher us into a corner. The food was wonderful: tarts with fresh sliced strawberries, a gelatin glace and a garnish of whipped cream; toasted tea buns, cheese toast or wheat germ muffins. Desserts served at the snack bar and restaurants were all freshly baked onsite. As well, there were butterscotch, chocolate, strawberry or pineapple ice cream sundaes.

The Hood

Although Gastown was being refurbished with paving stones and decorative lamp posts and Blood Alley and Maple Tree Square were newly gentrified, I didn't spend a lot of time there. Instead, working at Woodward's introduced me to the wonders and excitement of the Downtown Eastside. I never missed the Army and Navy spring shoe sale and shopped in the designer area.

The Chinatown shops on nearby Pender Street, with their bamboo fans, tables and stools, held great appeal. I would wander deep into the long, narrow Ming Wo Cookware Store to buy chopsticks, a wok and delicate blue and white rice bowls.

Ming Wo Cookware, 23 East Pender Street. The store opened in 1917. On January 8, 2020, the owners announced that the store would be closing.

The Army and Navy Department Store, 36 West Cordova Street entrance with the Woodward's W in the background. After more than 100 years in business, the store closed permanently in May 2020 due to the COVID-19 pandemic.

On Fridays, when Woodward's stayed open until 9:00, friends would sometimes meet me at the store, and we went to the local smoky pub and drank beer. Beer was five glasses for a dollar and served on round tables covered with red terry cloths secured with elastic. I was introduced to platters of Chinese food at the Green Door and steamed Alaska black cod at the Only Café on Hastings. The area always felt safe, even on dark winter nights.

Chunky Visits

Charles "Chunky" Woodward became president and chief executive officer of Woodward Stores Ltd. in 1957. During his era, the company added another 21 stores in B.C. and Alberta. From time to time, he visited the Food Floor. Word would go around. Be on your best behaviour. Stand tall. Adjust your uniform. Tidy your workstation. Straighten paper bags.

One of my occasional duties was to shop for Chunky. This always seemed to happen on an evening shift. Miss Schuhart would take me aside and give me the short list of groceries. The message, both overt and implicit, was "Get it right." I would cruise up and down the aisles carefully choosing the items on the list that included canned salmon, speciality teas, butter and mayonnaise. After I returned the order directly to Miss Schuhart, it would be hand delivered to the parking garage.

The next time I went shopping, I would buy some of the unfamiliar items from Chunky's list to try for myself.

Credit: MOV H2014.12.35h

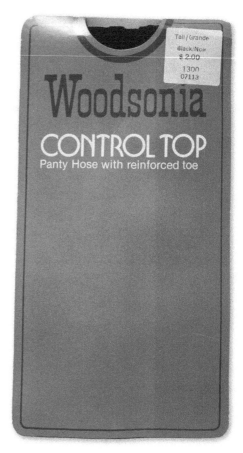

Beyond the Food Floor, there was hardware, jewelry, golf clubs and bags, cameras, textiles, furniture, floor coverings, tools, lamps, drapes and underwear, basketballs, trunks, tires, spectacles, shock absorbers and all manner of other things under various trade names held by the company.

When I started wearing hose, they were nylons held up with uncomfortable garter hooks. During the 1960s, new manufacturing technology resulted in the much more comfortable pantyhose. They were especially popular as hemlines rose to over the knee or even miniskirts. Luckily, pantyhose was one of the many items Woodward's produced to sell for $1.49. Ladies stocked up on them as they tended to run or tear easily. I kept a stash for my workdays at Woodward's.

$1.49 Day

In Vancouver, $1.49 day was an institution. Eaton's, the Hudson's Bay, Fields, the Army and Navy and many other stores copied $1.49 Day, but Woodward's sale jingle "$1.49 Day Woodward's, $1.49 Day Tuesday" is still an earworm for many.

Crowds assembled at the doors. When they opened, the attendant had to step back to avoid the surge. Soon the lunch counters were full as even they had $1.49 Day specials.

As the crowds lined up outside the store, we braced for the onslaught. Paper bags were neatly stacked. I soon knew what was on sale by the volume coming through the till. Typically, items that sold for $2 were reduced, although some were only available for the sale. The meat and bakery department came up with novel groupings I remember as being challenging to figure out: 1 lb. sliced side bacon, 8 oz. chicken-style loaf, 8 oz. Savoy loaf, all for $1.49; 1 jelly roll, 6 cinnamon buns, 1 chocolate brownie, all for $1.49

The steady stream of customers picked up as the day moved on. Before you knew it, it was lunch time. And then the day was over, having flown by with no time to notice tired feet or legs.

An ad from December 1, 1969 for the last $1.49 Day before Christmas, an extremely popular sale for families on a budget, lists a huge array of items including many for kids, such as: hockey sticks with fiberglass blades, Hot Wheel cars, Tonka lowboy truck, model car kits, soccer balls, and footballs.

The Trim-a-Home Shop featured: 7 outdoor light set $1.49; 15 indoor light set $1.49; Vinyl holly wreath $1.49; Christmas cards solid pack of 25 cards, 2 for $1.49; Woodward's bow pack of 36 bows, Christmas colours, 2 for $1.49; Woodward's black-and-white film in popular sizes 620, 120 and F127 5 for $1.49; Rich dark or light Christmas cake, ½ slab $1.49.

China Teacups

On the fourth floor, Woodward's carried a large selection of English bone china from such prestigious companies as Wedgewood, Royal Doulton and Royal Worcester. One set of dishes held a special place in many homes as they were available on $1.49 Days. Decorated with sprays of pink roses with grey petals, they are as comforting as a cup of tea on a drizzly Vancouver afternoon and filled many kitchen cupboards in Western Canada. The gold-rimmed items were especially attractive as Johnson Brothers gained Royal Warrants from both the Queen and Queen Mother, making them even more appealing to a large segment of the population. Remnants of the once ubiquitous set of Johnson Brothers dishes are now sold in thrift shops and antique stores for more than their original price.

Christmas

The Woodward's Christmas window display with lights and mechanized puppets were the place to visit for many in Vancouver. Reindeer pranced across the awning on Hastings Street while bowers of bows and holly festooned the pillars inside. Now, each year the puppets peak out over the harbour and Stanley Park from Canada Place as a legacy of the store.

The Beacon, the Woodward's in-house newsletter was published four times a year. This image from Christmas 1967 shows the stairs leading to the Food Floor.

Woodward's Christmas display at Canada Place.

Christmas was a busy time on the Food Floor. A department associated with the Food Floor was dedicated to shipping Christmas parcels to Great Britain. These were, I was told, started after the Second World War. Treats from Canada including tins of Pacific salmon, dried fruit from the Okanagan and other delicacies that were wrapped and shipped. Some of the long-time employees worked behind the scenes in this special shipping area.

Early in the season, we went to a Food Floor staff Christmas lunch party, a Chinese buffet in the Lotus Hotel at the corner of Abbott and Pender Streets. Miss Schuhart and Miss Martin, her assistant, would take us in shifts for an extended lunch hour. On Christmas Eve, we were sent home early once customers became sparse in the store.

The author (l) visited Santa in 1953 with her brothers Paul and Bill. Personal family collection.

Somewhat Indecent Exposures

Every year, each store held what was called Old-Fashioned Day. Women wore elaborate hats and long dresses. Men sported vests and straw boater hats reminiscent of those worn by barbershop quartets. There was music and various historical exhibits in honour of the day. The staff—especially, I suspect, the full-time regulars—embraced the event with enthusiasm. One year, I was scheduled to work on Old-Fashioned Day, and I wore a full-length red cotton dress I had made. It had long sleeves and, I thought,

Old-Fashioned Days, The Beacon, July, August 1967.

a modest neckline that showed no cleavage. Miss Schuhart, it seemed, was not quite sure and mumbled that perhaps I should wear a t-shirt underneath but, instead, let me proceed to my till.

Woodward's had many loyal customers who came each day for coffee or snacks and to meet with friends. They bought mini donuts, malts or hot dogs and spent time in the warmth of the store. Lynda Welch (Walton), a grocery wrapper when I worked there, recalls one time when Miss Schuhart was walking by and noticed a group of elderly men milling about at the snack bar. They seemed to be enjoying the view as the young female employees bent over to retrieve delivery boxes from under the wrapping area. She ordered all the young women to immediately leave the floor and get new longer uniforms. This was, of course, the era of the miniskirt.

The King of the Hippies

One day, as I arrived at work, we were asked to gather around Miss Schuhart at the podium. She was visibly upset and warned us that there was a potential invasion of the Food Floor led by the King of the Hippies and his followers. We were all to be on the lookout.

My friends and I suppressed a laugh; do hippies have kings, I thought?

Clearly Miss Schuhart was profoundly serious in her concerns. In his book *City of Love and Revolution*, Lawrence Aronsen (p. 116) describes a "sip-in" at the Hudson's Bay cafeteria on Saturday, May 8, 1970, when long-haired "Yippies" spent a few hours drinking coffee as a result of perceived discrimination by store security guards. I would have been working at Woodward's that day. Miss Schuhart and the management were reasonably concerned that they would move on from the Bay to Woodward's.

To some, hippies wore bell-bottom pants and beads and had long hair and were somewhat threatening. I had a much more nuanced view of so-called hippies. It was a tumultuous time. In July 1967, riots rocked Detroit, Washington, LA and Baltimore. Martin Luther King and Bobby Kennedy were murdered in 1968. The war raged on in Vietnam, and civil unrest spilled across the border, as did draft dodgers and deserters. It was an uncertain world, and the cold war between the USA and USSR continued. There were many front-page stories about Charles Manson.

There was also unrest on campus. On October 24, 1968, Jerry Rubin, a US Yippie, visited UBC. The America election was on, and he was promoting a pig as candidate. He addressed students and then moved on to occupy the Faculty Club. After I saw him speak on the plaza, I went to my English class rather than follow him to occupy the Faculty Club.

While it was time of anxiety and distress, it was also a time of excitement and idealism, a desire for independence, love and peace, social justice and concern for the environment. Youth were on the move, hitchhiking across the country. Vancouver was considered the "hippie capital of Canada," and Kitsilano became the

This City of Vancouver image of Abbott and Hastings Streets (circa 1981) shows Fields store on the right. Credit: CVA 772-58.

centre of the so-called counterculture. By 1967, long hair, peasant skirts, beads and sandals were the norm. In 1970, I lived in a two-bedroom plus den apartment at Third Avenue and Maple with two girlfriends, one who worked as a clerk at the Bay.

During these years, the music was magical and a big part of the cultural scene. The first concert I attended was the Beatles at Empire Stadium on August 22, 1964. I was high in the stands far above the screaming fans who rushed the stage, causing the concert to be cut short after only 29 minutes. Sonny and Cher played at the Queen Elizabeth Theatre. My friend Judy and I ran to the stage door hoping to catch a glimpse of them. I was in the crowd with my brother when Jimi Hendrix played at the Pacific Coliseum, and to see Blind Faith, including Eric Clapton and Ginger Baker; Jethro Tull, Country Joe and the Fish and many other groups. A young Gordon Lightfoot was a regular in the Student Union Building at UBC, and I saw him several times, lining up early to get a front-row seat. There were the Easter Be-ins and the Strawberry Mountain Festival. I loved them all. And Woodward's Concert Box Office was conveniently located at the store.

Miss Schuhart's fear of the invasion of the Food Floor by the King of the Hippies and his followers seemed greatly exaggerated.

The End of the Day

By the end of the day, my feet were sore. The smell of cans and onions on my hands never went away. I went back up the three floors to the changeroom, then down a set of stairs at the rear of the store. Staff spilled out onto Cordova Street from a door not accessible to the public.

Near the place where the old staff exit was, Woodwards' with a misplaced apostrophe is embedded in the sidewalk. Perhaps the apostrophe is not misplaced but instead reflects the different Woodward's that existed and exists today. This has been my story of Woodward's.

Acknowledgments

Violet Molnar, Barbara Mathias, VPL Special Collections, Arleen and Jack Mar, Lauralyn ÓRaghallaigh, the Woodward's Former Employees Facebook group, Clinton Lee, Sam Corea, Ray Piesciuk, Michael Kluckner, Douglas Shields, Robert McLachlan, Lynda Welch (Walton), Jim Cadwaladr, City of Vancouver Archives, Museum of Vancouver, and the Vancouver Public Library. I would especially like to thank book designer John McKercher and editor Judith Brand for their creativity and professionalism.

References

Books

Aronsen, Lawrence. *City of Love and Revolution: Vancouver in the Sixties*. Vancouver, New Star Books, 2010.

Brun, Mona. *Cooking with Mona: The Original Woodward's Cookbook*. Vancouver, Whitecap Books, Revised ed., 2003.

Davis, Chuck. *The Chuck Davis History of Metropolitan Vancouver*. Madera Park, B.C., Harbour Publishing, 2011.

Douglas, Stan. *Stan Douglas: Abbott & Cordova, 7 August 1971*. Vancouver, Arsenal Pulp Press, 2011.

Douglas, Stan and Reid Shier, ed. *Stan Douglas: Every Building on 100 West Hastings*. Vancouver, Arsenal Pulp Press, 2002.

Enright, Robert, ed. *Body Heat: The Story of the Woodward's Redevelopment*. Blue Imprint, 2010.

Kluckner, Michael and John Atkin. *Heritage Walks Around Vancouver*. Vancouver, Whitecap Books, 1992.

Other Printed Material

Thompson, Lindsay. *The Social Life of Things: A Case Study of the Woodward's Department Store*. Vancouver, University of British Columbia, Faculty of Graduate Studies, April 2005.

Vancouver Sun, Classified Advertisements. Vancouver, December 14, 1967, p. 64.

Internet

Russwurm, Lani. Gastown. *The Canadian Encyclopedia*. www.bing.com /search?q=canadian+encyclopedia&form=EDGSPH&mkt=en-ca &httpsmsn=1&plvar=0&refig=cdb15ba998d642cf9690ae2c730fb139& sp=1&qs=HS&pq=ca&sc=8-2&cvid=cdb15ba998d642cf9690ae2c730fb 139&cc=CA&setlang=en-GB. October 27, 2017 and edited November 21, 2017. Retrieved August 22, 2019

McManus, Theresa. "Memories of Woodward's flourish." www.newwest
 record.ca/news/memories-of-woodward-s-flourish-1.598747. Retrieved
 September 8, 2009.

http://vancouverhistory.ca/chronology1968.htm. Retrieved October 19.
 2019.

https://en.wikipedia.org/wiki/Johnson_Brothers#Restructuring_(1960
 –2000). Retrieved October 26, 2019.

https://en.wikipedia.org/wiki/Pantyhose. Retrieved November 6, 2019.

https://historyofrights.ca/encyclopaedia/main-events/1971-gastown-riot/.
 Retrieved January 15, 2020.

https://vancouverpolicemuseum.ca/gastown-riots-1971/. Retrieved January 15, 2020.

www.hbcheritage.ca/history/acquisitions/woodwards-stores-ltd.
 Retrieved January 25, 2020.

rerides.ca/boot-of-the-day/2015/09/paris-logging-boots/. Retrieved April
 13, 2020.

Woodward's Department Store and Food Floor Private Facebook group.

wikipedia.org/wiki/McDonald%27s_Canada. Retrieved April 25, 2020.

www.thedepartmentstoremuseum.org. Retrieved July 5, 2019; April 4,
 2020.

https://www.msn.com/en-ca/news/canada/covid-19-end-of-an-era-as
 -army-and-navy-closes-after-101-years/ar-BB13QCSg?ocid=spartandhp.
 Retrieved May 10, 2020.

Index

About the Author

Margaret Cadwaladr, MA is a writer, public speaker and publisher who was born in Vancouver B.C and graduated from UBC. Her interests include life writing and memoir. This is her third book. Contact Margaret at Foodfloor67@gmail.com

Author website: https://www.foodfloordays.com.

Also by Madrona Books & Publishing:

In Veronica's Garden: The Social History of the Milner Gardens and Woodland by Margaret Cadwaladr. A new expanded edition of the Canadian best-seller was published in 2018.

Speed's War: A Canadian Soldier's Memoir of World War II by George A. Reid

Come Back Judy Baba: Memoirs of India by Mary Hargreaves Norbury and Judy Norbury

9 781999 546519